COLOR THRU HISTORY

THE PEOPLE OF THE COMPUTER AGE

I0105864

PICTURE BOOK SUPPLEMENT

Learn & Color Books
  an imprint of Master Design Marketing, LLC
  30 N Gould St, Ste R
  Sheridan, WY 82801
  www.LearnAndColor.com

For information about special discounts available for bulk purchases, sales promotions, fund-raising and educational needs, contact Learn & Color Books Company Sales at sales@LearnAndColor.com.

ISBN: 978-1-947482-58-6 (paperback)
ISBN: 978-1-947482-59-3 (hardback)
ISBN: 978-1-947482-60-9 (ebook)

Cover and interior design by Faithe F Thomas
Research by Caitlyn F Williams
Images are © Master Design Marketing, LLC

Look for the Scottish Flag somewhere in each of our books.

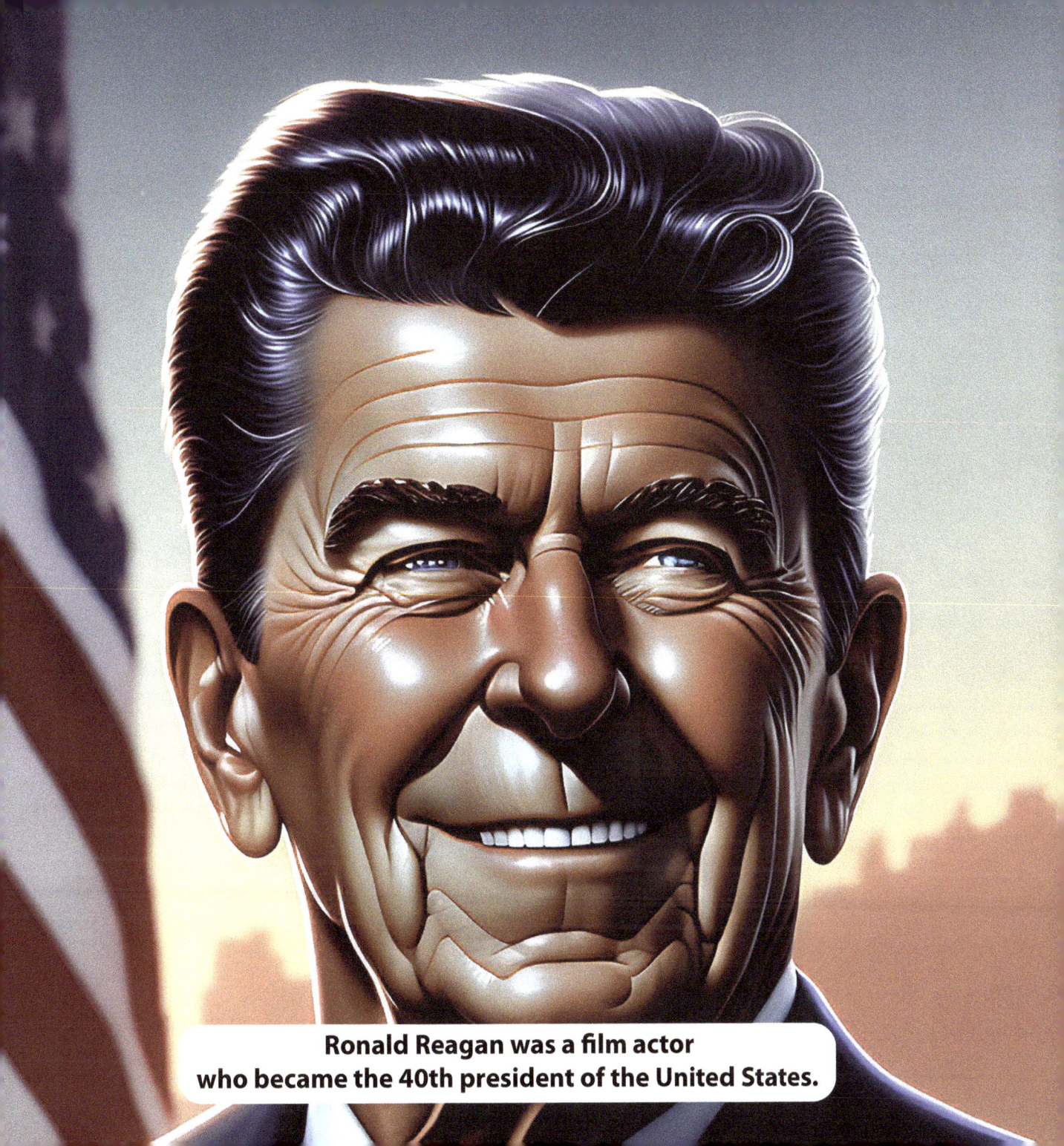

Ronald Reagan was a film actor
who became the 40th president of the United States.

Sam Walton founded Walmart and became the richest man in America for a time.

Pope John Paul II (Karol Józef Wojtyla) was the Pope from 1978 to 2005.
His wish was for Jews, Muslims, and Christians to work together.

Neil Armstrong was the first person to walk on the moon. He said, "That's one small step for man, one giant leap for mankind."

Desmond Tutu was a South African Anglican bishop known for his work in helping the black people of South Africa.

Mikhail Gorbachev was the last leader of the former Soviet Union. He helped end the Cold War with the West.

Stephen Hawking was an English scientist whose work advanced our understanding of black holes and quantum mechanics.

George W. Bush was the 43rd president of the United States. He was president during the attacks of the Twin Towers.

Bill Clinton was the 42nd president of the United States. He is married to Hillary Rodham Clinton.

Steven Spielberg is an American filmmaker known for directing films such as *Jaws, Close Encounters, Raiders of the Lost Ark, E.T.,* and *Jurrasic Park.*

Donald Trump is a businessman, TV personality, and the 45th president of the United States.

Craig Venter is an American scientist who led the first team to sequence the human DNA.

Benjamin Netanyahu was the first Israeli Prime Minister born in Israel.

Richard Branson is an English businessman and founder of Virgin Group, which controls more than 400 companies.

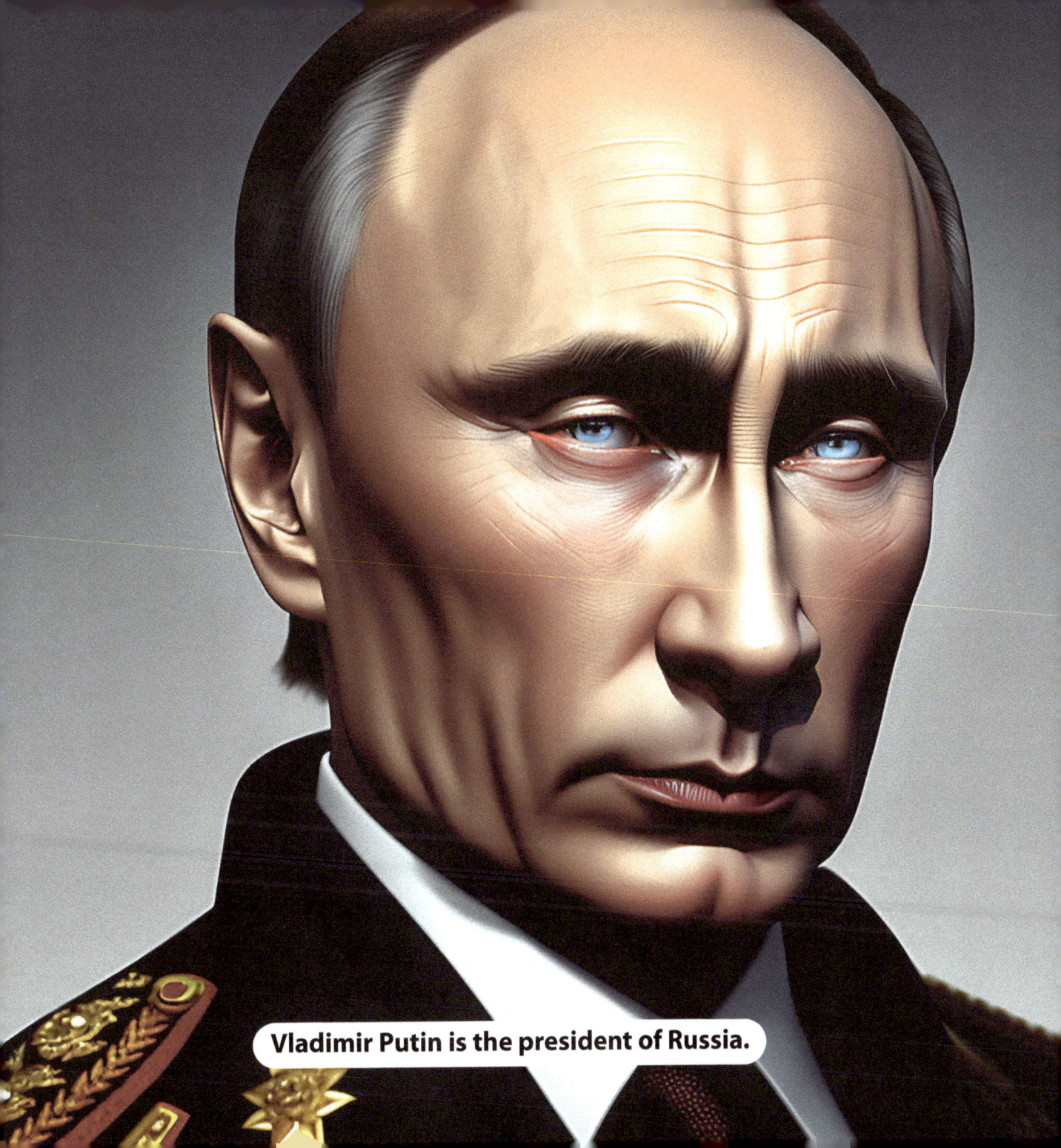
Vladimir Putin is the president of Russia.

Xi Jinping is the leader of the Communist Party in the People's Republic of China.

Oprah Winfrey is an American businesswoman, actress, and producer.

Bill Gates is an American businessman and one of the founders of Microsoft Corporation.

Tim Berners-Lee is an English engineer best known as the inventor of the World Wide Web.

Steve Jobs was an American businessman who co-founded Apple Inc. He also helped develop Pixar, maker of the film *Toy Story*.

Osama bin Laden was the founder of al-Qaeda, a terrorist organization which allegedly caused the 9/11 attacks on New York City.

Diana, Princess of Wales, was the first wife of the current King of England and mother of Prince William and Prince Harry.

Barack Hussein Obama II was the
44th president of the United States.

Jeffrey Preston Bezos is an American entrepreneur who founded Amazon.com, Inc.

Jimmy Wales is an American internet entrepreneur known as the co-founder of the online encyclopedia, Wikipedia.

Tank Man is the nickname of the unidentified Chinese man who stopped a row of tanks in Tiananman Square on June 5, 1989.

Elon Musk is the founder of SpaceX, co-founder of Tesla, co-founder of Neuralink, founder of The Boring Company, co-founder of OpenAI, co-founder of Paypal, and owner of Twitter.

Sergey Brin and Larry Page are the founders of Google.

Kim Jong-un is the Supreme Leader of North Korea.

Mark Zuckerberg is an American entrepreneur and co-founder of Facebook.